"i dont believe in love. do you:

"i believe in love, its just never mutual"

forgetting the palm of your hand
why is it so hard
the way you were so
effortlessly
beautiful

aliza grace

it makes me sick
how in love i was with you

the thing is i was never in love with <u>you</u>

i was in love with a version of you
a version i made up

the man you will never be

aliza grace

you give all
your pieces away
and wonder why
you fall apart
so easily

you love me
all of me
even these demons
the ones deep in my soul
my darkest parts
the torment in my mind

and thats how love should be

wait for someone who loves you differently
the one who can see the fire in your soul
the child in your laugh
and the
ocean in your heart

you will find home in this human

maybe we just found forever
at the wrong time
and maybe someday
time will pull us back
together again

all i ever wanted
was to love you
and to be loved by you

but you had
to make that so
hard

aliza grace

i hate who youve became
you dont care about
how you make me feel anymore

did you ever really care

love isnt a choice
you dont get to choose
if that was the case
i wouldve stopped loving you
a long time ago

aliza grace

i really wish you well
if happiness wasnt with me
if i was the thing holding you back
its time i let go of you

this is me moving on

aliza grace

letting go of what could have been

such a painful thing to indulge in

aliza grace

growing up in a society
that can undress
women with their eyes

porn kills love

you are not the first
set of eyes
that i have confused
for home

but you were by far
the hardest to leave

enjoy
the
now

aliza grace

you are colours
i have never seen
the softness
i have never felt
flavors
i have never tasted

they will
leave
they always do
its just
a matter
of when

i forgot
what the
dream was
about

i just
remember seeing
your face

aliza grace

whats meant to stay
will stay

3am
laying in bed
alone
im left in tears
you are not here
beside of me
where you belong

i dont want to let go
yes i know
i have to
its been a year
365 days without your touch
im still keeping track
i have lost so much sleep

it doesnt get easier does it

aliza grace

kiss me each day
like its our very last
because one day
it will be

aliza grace

never let me
hold you back

"enough"

that word and wondering what it means

has kept me awake

longer then it should have

and the thought

why will i never be "enough" for you

its right in front of your face
the girl who will keep trying
keep breaking all of the rules
for you
an average guy
the guy i cant seem to get over

i guess your blind

i dont know what made you stand out
you just kinda exist

and i could write novels about how perfect you are
how i am so in love with your presence

.

falling in love with
someones potential
its such a terrible thing
to do

aliza grace

they say beauty is in the eye
of the beholder
but
i never felt beautiful
when i was with you

aliza grace

aliza grace

pain
its the only thing
that is totally
bonding us together

we are just human
capable of so much
yet we choose
the same cycle
hurt and get hurt

my heart hurts for the girl i was
a year ago

im proud of myself

i have came so far

emotional abuse
is the worst
personally
i would rather be
beaten
and dragged through
the dirt
then endure this

you have all the power
you need to be the
best version of yourself

block him
if you dont
youll keep viewing
his page
its gonna hurt so bad
to see him
with another girl
who isnt you
one that looks nothing
like you

aliza grace

you deserve love

lonely
something i never felt
with you

too bad you left

we are human
we feel pain
in the end
thats what draws
us closer
to one another
we desire to feel understood

reading old messages
crying to his favorite song
smelling his clothes
the ones you still have
looking at photos
trying to remember the
guy he was

its not gonna make him
come back

my mistake
i finally wanted to
be loved
by someone
a person who
loved me back

unfortunately
i chose the wrong
someone

i
cant
cry
you
back
or
you
would
already
be
back

im so mad at you
you made me hate you
and i used to love you
but
now i look at you
and i feel anger
you changed
what turned you
so bitter inside

please be easy
with my heart
all it knows is
hurt and pain

aliza grace

how can someone
be so beautiful
everything about you
is perfect
your my person
you
will
always
be my person

i forgot to tell you
i love you
how your hair falls
that certain way
your big eyes
how you can talk for hours
about the same thing
how you are so passionate
about giving
i love you

aliza grace

part of me hates you
the other part wants you
back

why does it have to be this way

what did i ever do to deserve this

i gave you all of my love

you gave me hurt

the truth is
i dont feel
anything for
you anymore

and i am
so glad

aliza grace

you look me
right in my eyes
square in my soul
and lie to me

what
made you
so cold

aliza grace

you never loved me
if you did
you would be here

but your not
your in another
girls bed

aliza grace

if its not
mutual
whats the point

take a good look at me
the girl *you* let walk
out the door
my voice makes mountains
tremble
you will look back
everyday
and regret
all of your actions

we were young
but it was real
wasnt it
even if we ended up
breaking each others hearts
we both really cared for one
another
you taught me
how to love
and how it feels to be loved

you taught me
how to love
and how it
feels to be loved

aliza grace

i used to see
love in your eyes

now its just
boredom

aliza grace

call me
if you miss me
because
i miss you too

it was never meant to
end this way

it was so real
we deserve another shot

aliza grace

<u>you are my best friend</u>
the love i have for you
will always be there
and nothing or
no one
could ever make that
change

aliza grace

the world needs you
your special
even if you havent
figured that out yet
you will one day
i promise

aliza grace

you cheated on me
and your mad i found out

the audacity

if it isnt me one day
tell me
dont break my heart
loving
another girl
when you sleep
next to me

aliza grace

i loved you so much
i dont know
how to love myself
now that your gone

aliza grace

meet me at midnight
when the rest
of the town is quiet
love away
my worries

aliza grace

this friendship
is the only reason
i believe in soulmates

aliza grace

at the end of the day
its just my body
searching for yours

aliza grace

missing you
comes
in waves
tonight
im drowning

aliza grace

i was loosing you somewhere between the lines of
who we once were and who we have become
i can feel you slowly drifting away from me as if
you have never truly held on
its tiring watching you become someone that i no
longer recognize
its a hard concept in becoming so familiar with
someone
just to one day only remember them in idle things
such as pictures and faint memories
you are all that i once was
all that i held onto
now i fear you are the worst version
of yourself

aliza grace

sometimes late at night
our memories sneak out of my eyes
and roll down my cheek

why does the girls
you follow
on social media
make me hurt so bad

because i know
you would pick them
over me
if it came down to
that

aliza grace

your eyes were
never only
on me

aliza grace

i want to be a girl
in the sense other girls are
they smell like summer
and always have the right
right words to say
poised and velvety
secure in their grace

their smiles are
innocent yet coy
and their body
compels instead of repels

even their tears
are enviable
delicately streaking
their soft pink cheeks
prom problems i wish to have

meanwhile ugly sobs
rock my broad shoulders
and harsh face
as i reconstruct
who i am
outside and inside
        just to have an ounce of their femininity

you left
and i
needed you

your gone
and i dont
need you

can you really say
that you felt nothing for
me

that we were nothing

aliza grace

missing you hurts
i dont want to
hurt anymore

so
can
you
just
come
back

aliza grace

you picked the pieces of my heart off the ground
and fitted them back together

your the boy who made my heart whole again
gave me a purpose to keep going

my heart

my support

aliza grace

she will never look
at you like
i looked at you

so full of love
for you

dont you dare
bother
crawling
back to me

when you realise
that

i had you
and i was happy

i have lost you
and im still
happy

tomorrow will be better
thats what i keep telling myself

then tomorrow comes
and its worse then yesterday

i keep hoping tomorrow
will be better

when will it be better

aliza grace

starting an argument
just to get attention
from you

i hope each night
when you lay
your head
on your pillow
its my face you see

i hope its my name
that accidentally rolls off your
tongue when your with her

i hope its my scent
thats always lingering
on all the hoodies
i gave back to you

i hope theres always pieces
of me
haunting you

aliza grace

when you get food
at the places we got food
do you think of me

because i think of you

when you hear those songs on the radio
the ones i blasted with the windows down
do you think of me

because i think of you

when you go to the grocery store and see
my favorite foods
the ones you would always buy for me
do you still think of me

because i think of you
i cant eat those foods now

im always thinking of you
do you ever think of me too?

sadness is a black hole
im so lost in

aliza grace

i bet your dog misses me

aliza grace

i bet your cat misses me

why am i still
crying over
you

aliza grace

i dont want
to hurt
anymore

aliza grace

im glad we happened
even if we ended
even though we ended badly
there was once a time we were so happy
with each other
and for that
im thankful

thank you
for giving it
another chance
we dont work
thats obvious now
but thank you
for trying again
for me

aliza grace

dont call her
what you used
to call me

aliza grace

im still
hoping
its just
me and you
in the
end

aliza grace

im trapped between
not needing you
and crying for you to
come back

what an awful place to be

sometimes
in sad
and i
dont know
why

aliza grace

does she
treat you
better
than i
did?

aliza grace

it hurts
to remember how
close we were back then

aliza grace

our
goodbye
hurt

the memories
hurt more

overthinking
something i always do
somehow its calming really

other times it destroys me
either way i cant stop

aliza grace

maybe one day
ill be everything you
want
the girl you
need

I wanna take you everywhere and spoil you and do cute things with you and take pictures together and hold hands and show you off to the world and share sunsets and car rides and drinks together and cute lil kisses on your nose and concerts and cool asf museums and aquariums and go to random dumb places like home depot just bc we can idk

aliza grace

silence
can
sometimes
hold
all
the
answers
you
need
to
hear

sometimes
i catch myself
still thinking
about you
and my heart breaks
again
even now

aliza grace

i hope you think of me
today
tomorrow
in a year
i hope you think of me

my lips on yours make me feel whole.

where did my other half go?

my lips on yours made me feel whole.

where did my other half go?

aliza grace

youll never really forget
youll just be okay with remembering

aliza grace

i love you
more then i have
ever loved myself

its you
im convinced
it will always be you

aliza grace

i love you
in this lifetime
and every one after

aliza grace

find me
in every lifetime
my love

aliza grace

its you
thats perfect for me

aliza grace

i wanted
you
to only
want me

you wanted her instead

in the
end
its me and you
and i know
we got this

stop making excuses
if you truly wanted to be here
with me
you would
pain and simple
as that

but guess what
your not
here with me
you dont want to be
plain as that

aliza grace

you ripped my heart
out of my chest
and stomped on it

you make me
feel like i will
be okay

i hate the feeling
when you see something
and your heart sinks

aliza grace

the reason i keep
my feelings to myself
is because i cant explain them

aliza grace

to see a rainbow
be paitent
and wait
on the rain

mind: he is not worth your time

heart: you dont know him like i do

aliza grace

i am learning to rest and heal
that is always enough

aliza grace

you know how much it
hurts me but you do it anyway

aliza grace

sometimes it takes the worst pain
to bring about the best change

aliza grace

imagine hurting
the girl
God sent you

i want to love my body
and i do to some extent
i want to love it fully
but i cant

aliza grace

i look at my bed
and im reminded of you
all the memories flood my mind
how i would cry myself to sleep
in your arms

ironic how i cry by myself now

aliza grace

you miss me
but never enough
to call
never enough to text me
never enough
to stop by
my house and see me

you dont miss me

you say your sorry for
leaving
and i half way believe you
if you were sorry
why did you do it
if your so in love with me
why did you leave
only to return
and confuse me

i dont know your mind
i dont know what you are thinking
please dont leave again
i need you

aliza grace

turn around
right now
come back to me
it doesnt have to be this way
it cant end this way

why cant this just be a bad dream

aliza grace

i think of you
less
and less

you were my
one in a million
you said goodbye
too early

aliza grace

i will always cherish
the time you gave me

aliza grace

now
your just
a story i will
tell my kids when
they ask about heartbreak

aliza grace

i dont think i will ever
feel whole again

aliza grace

we really had all
the potential to work out

it was you that gave up

aliza grace

ill take you back
come back

dear reader

thank you for giving my book
a chance
i hope that you enjoy
and that the words resonate
in some way

please leave a review
on amazon

you are beautiful and so worthy
just know whatever it is
it gets better
i promise

until next time
aliza

aliza grace